Golden Retrievers

and Other Sporting Dogs

Editor in Chief: Paul A. Kobasa
Supplementary Publications: Lisa Kwon, Christine Sullivan, Scott Thomas
Research: Mike Barr, Timothy J. Breslin, Cheryl Graham, Barbara Lightner, Loranne Shields
Graphics and Design: Kathy Creech, Sandra Dyrlund, Charlene Epple, Tom Evans
Permissions: Janet Peterson
Indexing: David Pofelski
Prepress and Manufacturing: Anne Dillon, Carma Fazio, Anne Fritzinger, Steven Hueppchen,
    Tina Ramirez
Writer: Robert N. Knight

For information about other World Book publications, visit our Web site at http://www.worldbook.com or call 1-800-WORLDBK (967-5325).

For information about sales to schools and libraries, call 1-800-975-3250 (United States); 1-800-837-5365 (Canada).

World Book, Inc.
233 N. Michigan Avenue
Chicago, IL 60601
U.S.A.

Library of Congress Cataloging-in-Publication Data

Golden retrievers and other sporting dogs.
     p. cm. -- (World Book's animals of the world)
   Summary: "An introduction to Golden Retrievers and Other Sporting
Dogs, presented in a highly illustrated, question and answer format.
Features include fun facts, glossary, resource list, index, and
scientific classification list"--Provided by publisher.
   Includes bibliographical references and index.
   ISBN-13: 978-0-7166-1328-2
   ISBN-10: 0-7166-1328-X
   1. Golden retriever--Miscellanea--Juvenile literature. 2. Hunting
dogs--Miscellanea--Juvenile literature. I. World Book, Inc. II.
Series.
SF429.G63G55 2007
636.752'7—dc22
                              2006017320

Printed in Malaysia
1 2 3 4 5 6 7 8 09 08 07 06

Picture Acknowledgements: Cover: © Mark Raycroft, Minden Pictures; © Lynn M. Stone.

© Gemstone/Alamy Images 19; © Rhonda Brenza, As Good as Gold (Golden Retriever Rescue of Northern Illinois) 23; *Plover Shooting* by Francis Barlow, oil on canvas, Private Collection (Bridgeman Art Library) 9; © Mindy Chung, Shutterstock 57; © Corbis 61; © Mitsuaki Iwago, Minden Pictures 37; © Andrew Linscott, Alamy Images 55; © Carolyn A. McKeone 27; © Tracy Morgan, Dorling Kindersley 29; © William H. Mullins, Photo Researchers 21; © Robert Pearcy, Animals Animals 45; © Dave Porter, Alamy Images 5, 43; © Mike Powell, Getty Images 35; © Mark Raycroft, Minden Pictures 4, 7, 49, 51; © Chin Kit Sen, Shutterstock 5, 47; © Frank Siteman, PhotoEdit 31; © Peter Skinner, Photo Researchers 41, © Lynn M. Stone 15, 17; © Lynn M. Stone, Nature Picture Library 39; © age fotostock/SuperStock 25; © Mauritius/SuperStock 33, © Purestock/SuperStock 59; © Seth Wenig, Reuters/Landov 3, 53.

Illustrations: WORLD BOOK illustration by John Fleck 13.

Golden Retrievers

and Other Sporting Dogs

World Book, Inc.
a Scott Fetzer company
Chicago

Contents

What Is a Sporting Dog?

Long ago in England, *sporting* meant *hunting for sport*. In ancient times, hunters trained falcons to help them find and catch game (animals being hunted). Eventually, people began training dogs to help them hunt. Over time, hunters bred dogs to produce better hunting dogs. Four kinds of sporting dogs—pointers, retrievers, setters, and spaniels— were developed to help those hunting with guns.

- Pointers look for game. When they find it, they stand still and point with snout (nose) and paw.

- Retrievers, such as goldens, retrieve, or fetch and bring back, birds that have been shot.

- Setters find game birds and creep up on them to scare, or set, them in place for the hunter.

- Spaniels are trained to do a variety of the hunting tasks listed above.

Together, these kinds of dogs make up the group that we call sporting dogs today.

A golden retriever

7

How Did Breeds of Sporting Dogs Develop?

A breed is a group of animals that have the same type of ancestors. Because many of the breeds of sporting dogs arose many centuries ago, we know little about their early development.

One of the earliest sources about dogs is a book published in London in 1570 by a physician named John Caius. In his book, *Of English Dogs,* Caius listed and described the types of dogs then living in England. He identified setters, water spaniels, and land spaniels. The water spaniels were similar to retrievers today.

Art is another source of information about what dogs were like in the past. Artists working long ago sometimes featured or included dogs in their paintings. Artists often painted spaniels. *Spaniel* means *from Spain,* so historians believe that these dogs came to England from Spain.

A painting from the 1600's shows a spaniel hunting

9

When and Where Did the Golden Retriever Breed First Appear?

Dudley Coutts Marjoribanks *(MARSH banks)* lived from 1820 to 1894. He was a hunting sportsman and a dog lover. Marjoribanks raised dogs on his estate, called Guisachan (pronounced *KUSH guhn*), near the village of Tomich in Scotland. Marjoribanks searched the countryside for special dogs from which to breed the best litters of puppies.

One day, Marjoribanks saw a retriever with a yellow coat. He immediately bought that dog and named it Nous *(noos)*. Nous became the father of a litter of yellow puppies. The mother was a water spaniel named Belle. Their pups, born in 1868, started the line of dogs we call golden retrievers, or goldens.

Dogs born of the line founded by Belle and Nous were taken to the United States and had puppies. In 1932, the American Kennel Club (AKC), the major registry of purebred dogs in the United States, recognized the golden retriever.

Map showing the village in Scotland where the golden retriever developed

Arctic Ocean

North America

Asia

Tomich, Scotland

Europe

Atlantic Ocean

Africa

South America

Equator

What Does a Golden Look Like?

A golden retriever is a medium-sized dog. A mature golden male stands about 2 feet (0.6 meter) high at the shoulder; a female would usually be a little smaller. The golden's long, muscular legs make up nearly half that height.

Goldens have yellowish coats of varying colors. Some have light, cream-colored coats and others have more reddish coats.

The golden's coat is very thick and fluffy. The golden is definitely a long-haired dog. Golden experts and groomers describe the especially long hair on the golden's chest, belly, at the back of the legs, and on the tail as "feathering."

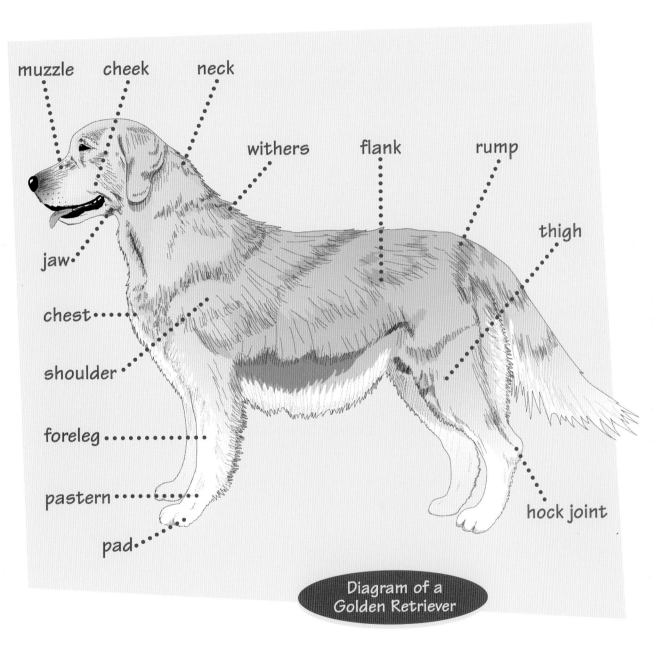

muzzle cheek neck

withers flank rump

jaw

thigh

chest

shoulder

foreleg

pastern

hock joint

pad

Diagram of a
Golden Retriever

What Kind of Personality Might a Golden Have?

Dogs within a breed are not exactly alike, of course, but often they do share many personality traits.

Most people agree that golden retrievers are usually outgoing, friendly, playful dogs. Goldens like being around people and are fun-loving dogs. Dogs from this breed, however, are happier and more secure when they have been carefully trained.

Most golden owners end up with happy, lovable dogs. It's important to remember, though, that a dog's personality is partly formed by the way it is treated and trained. Owners have a responsibility to provide a home in which their goldens will be able to be happy.

A friendly
golden retriever

Is a Golden Retriever the Dog for You?

You might think that anyone would want a golden retriever. But, in fact, these wonderful dogs aren't for everyone. There are some good reasons to choose a dog that is not a golden. Some people, for instance, have a small home. They might need a smaller dog that will be comfortable in tight spaces. Further, because goldens have thick coats and shed a lot of fur, people who are particular about housekeeping may want a dog that sheds less.

Finally, though no one should ignore any pet, some breeds of dogs can better accept being alone for longer periods of time. Goldens are not, however, one of those breeds. Golden retrievers need human companionship and lots of exercise and play, especially outdoors. People who are away from home a lot probably shouldn't choose a golden.

The American Kennel Club recognizes more than 150 dog breeds and there are also many kinds of mixed-breed dogs. People who want a dog that is right for them can usually find one.

An active golden runs
through the water

17

What Should You Look for When Choosing a Golden Puppy?

One way to start would be to find a good breeder of golden retrievers. A place to look is on the Web sites of the American Kennel Club (AKC), the Golden Retriever Club of America (GRCA), or the Golden Retriever Club of Canada (GRCC). See page 64 for the Internet addresses of these organizations.

Good breeders are careful when selecting a male and female dog for breeding. They try to screen out dogs with health problems that could get passed on to puppies.

Once you've found a good breeder, what should you look for in a litter of puppies? Trust your feelings. Which puppy do you especially like? Which puppy seems curious about you? If color is an issue, examine the puppies' ears. Most puppies darken as they grow, but their ears are usually closest to their grown-up color.

Golden retriever
puppies

19

Should You Get an Older Golden Instead of a Puppy?

Puppies are fun and adorable, but they are not for everyone. They are full of bounce and energy at every waking moment. They make messes and need a lot more attention than older dogs. Whether to get a puppy or a mature dog is probably a decision best left to the adults in your family. Raising and training a puppy can be a great family project, but everyone must be willing to accept the challenge.

Fully grown goldens are calmer and more settled, but they are just as lovable as puppies. Further, grown dogs are usually already housetrained (trained to relieve themselves outside of the house). Breeders of golden retrievers may have older dogs for sale as well as puppies.

An older golden

Should You Consider a Rescue Golden?

Not everyone who gets a pet can keep it for the pet's entire life. Sometimes dogs are abandoned, or left behind, by owners. And, sometimes dogs get lost.

Fortunately, there are rescue organizations today for most dog breeds. Often, rescue volunteers place abandoned dogs in foster homes while they try to find each dog a permanent home.

Golden retrievers have a talent for adapting to new situations. Most of the time, rescue goldens accept their new owners and continue being happy, lovable pets.

If a puppy isn't practical for your family, you might want to discuss getting a golden retriever from a rescue organization. Most of these organizations are set up on a local or state basis. (Some of the Web sites on page 64 of this book list groups that are active in golden rescue.)

Goldens at a
rescue organization
await a home

23

What Does a Golden Retriever Eat?

Like people, dogs need to eat a diet that will keep them healthy. Dogs need different nutrients, or nourishing things, than people do. That's why it is best for a dog to eat dog food, instead of being fed on table scraps (human food). Your veterinarian can suggest a type of dog food that is just right for your dog.

You might think that anything that is safe for you to eat is safe for your dog, but that is just not true. Some people foods are actually poisonous to dogs. For example, chocolate can make dogs sick or even kill them. Onions, grapes, and raisins are also very bad for dogs. Before you give a dog anything other than dog food to eat, make sure it is safe.

In addition to food, fresh drinking water must be available to a dog at all times. Water is important to your pet's health.

Dog food is best
for a golden

Where Should a Golden Sleep?

Dogs like routine, that is, they like for things to stay much the same from day to day. Sticking to one sleeping place and routine every night helps your dog feel safe and secure.

Some dog owners buy a bed for their dog. A good dog bed should be cushioned and it should be in a safe, quiet place.

Many dog experts say that a dog should have its own crate. This crate gives a dog a place to sleep and to feel safe. A dog crate is a big box with a large door. It might be made of metal wire or of heavy plastic with a lot of air holes. You can make a cozy sleeping area inside a dog crate by putting soft bedding inside.

Some dogs sleep in their owner's bed. Before you let your golden sleep with you, however, you should ask a grown-up. You may not sleep as soundly with your dog in bed with you. Furthermore, once you've let your dog sleep with you, it won't be easy to keep it out of your bed if you should later change your mind about sharing.

A golden in its crate

27

How Do You Groom a Golden?

The "golden" in "golden retriever" describes the dog's thick, rich coat of shiny gold. Actually, a golden's coat has two layers. The coat you see is the outer coat, made up of long "guard hairs." These hairs contain an oil that repels (pushes away) water, so the outer coat is rather like a raincoat. The hidden, inner coat is made up of soft, downy fur that helps the dog keep warm in cold weather. Dogs shed most of their inner coat of fine, wispy hairs in the spring.

A golden's coat needs regular grooming to look and be its best. A golden should be brushed thoroughly once or twice a week. Your veterinarian or groomer can help your family choose the right combs, brushes, and other grooming tools.

Your dog's nails, teeth, and ears need to be cared for as well. And its coat and skin must be kept free of fleas and ticks. Your vet or groomer can help you with these tasks, too.

The dense coat of a
golden retriever

What About Training a Golden?

Sometimes, adorable puppies grow up to be big, annoying, uncontrollable dogs. This happens when a puppy is not properly trained.

To begin with, every dog needs to learn who is boss. Long ago, when dogs were wild, they lived, worked, and played in groups called packs. Every dog pack had a lead dog that was "the boss." Your dog still wants to know who is boss and that should be the person or people who will train it.

Dog experts rate golden retrievers as one of the most trainable dog breeds. Goldens like to learn. They just need to be guided in the right direction. You can get help training your dog from an expert at a dog obedience school. To find out about dog obedience schools in your area, check with your veterinarian or the local chapter of a golden retriever club.

Goldens are a very trainable dog

What Kinds of Exercise or Play Are Needed?

Spending all day in front of the television or in an easy chair will not satisfy a healthy, young or middle-aged golden. Remember that goldens were bred to go hunting. They still like being outside. They run and play to work off all that sporting-dog energy.

Don't forget that word "retriever." One of the games your golden will enjoy most is retrieving, or fetching, balls, sticks, and Frisbees. Just make sure that whatever you throw for your dog is too big to be swallowed.

Dog experts say that mature goldens need at least one hour of exercise over the course of each day. Puppies don't need as much scheduled exercise. They'll work off their energy with all kinds of puppy play and mischief.

Goldens love to
run and play

Do Goldens Like Water?

Golden retrievers were bred to splash through ponds to retrieve birds for hunters. Most goldens enjoy water, and that makes bathing a golden a lot easier and more pleasant than it would be with many other breeds.

Goldens enjoy swimming, and they are fine swimmers. At pet stores, you can buy floating rubber toys or toys on a rope for your dog to retrieve from water. Of course, that's only if you have a fresh, clear lake or pond available.

Your golden must only be allowed to swim in a safe, clean body of water. Always follow this rule: Let adults decide when it's safe for your dog— or you—to go swimming.

After your dog swims or bathes, take the time to dry its coat well with a big, fluffy towel. Leaving its coat wet for too long could cause the dog to have skin problems.

A golden retriever swimming

How Can You Help a Golden Care for Its Young?

If your family has a golden mother with a litter, or if friends or relatives do, you need to know how to behave around the dogs. A mother dog naturally protects her young. If she thinks that the pups are under threat, she may snarl or try to bite. That's why it's important to approach a litter of puppies in the right way. Never do so without permission of an adult who is present. When you get close to the dogs, keep your voice quiet and don't make any sudden moves.

A mother dog provides all the things her pups need. However, if a pup gets away from the litter box and seems lost, you may gently take it back. Very young puppies can become dangerously chilled if they get in cool drafts, so a puppy needs to be in a warm place with its mother.

A golden mother
with her puppies

Are There Special Organizations for Golden Owners?

You've already read about the Golden Retriever Clubs of America (GRCA) and of Canada (GRCC). The GRCA was formed in 1938 and the GRCC in 1958. Both groups sponsor many programs and events for goldens and their owners.

You can find out about local chapters of these clubs at their Web sites (see page 64 for the addresses). Your local chapter will have information about good breeders of golden retrievers in your area.

The GRCA Web site also maintains a list of rescue organizations across the United States. If you're thinking of getting a rescue dog, this is a good place to start.

The American Kennel Club also sponsors programs and events for all recognized dog breeds, including golden retrievers.

A golden retriever

How Do Goldens Help Blind People and Deaf People?

People who are blind can have a hard time moving from place to place. They cannot see people, bicycles, cars, or traffic signals, such as walk/don't walk signs. Specially trained dogs called dog guides, or seeing eye dogs, can do some of the seeing for blind people. This helps the blind get around for their daily activities. You can identify a guide dog by its special harness attached to a U-shaped handle.

When people started training and using dogs as guide dogs for the blind—about 80 years ago—they used mainly German shepherds. Today, most of the guide dogs are golden retrievers or Labrador retrievers (a breed closely related to the golden, see page 48), or a mix of the two breeds.

Some golden retrievers work as dog guides for people who are hearing impaired. These hearing dogs, or hearing ear dogs, listen for such noises as alarms. When such a noise sounds, a hearing dog gets its owner's attention right away.

A golden retriever
guide dog

What Are Some Other Sporting Dog Breeds?

Sporting dogs include pointers, retrievers, setters, and spaniels. These dogs were all bred to help hunters using guns. Breeds in this group are called gundogs in the United Kingdom.

Today, the American Kennel Club recognizes 26 separate breeds in the sporting group. That number will probably grow because new breeds come along every now and then.

On the following pages, you can learn more about four sporting dog breeds.

Weimaraners are a type of pointer in the sporting dog class

What Is an English Springer Spaniel?

To flush, or spring, birds is to cause birds hiding in the brush and bushes to fly out and leave their cover. Therefore, dogs that found and flushed game birds were called springers. The English springer spaniel developed from these dogs. The name "springer" spaniel was chosen by the Sporting Spaniel Society of Britain in 1902.

Like a golden retriever, the English springer spaniel has long hair with feathering on its belly, chest, and legs. This spaniel also has feathering on its ears. The springer spaniel's coat can be black-and-white or brown-and-white, sometimes with tan markings. The American Kennel Club standards state an English springer spaniel should be between 19 to 20 inches (48 to 51 centimeters) tall at the shoulder.

English springer spaniels are outgoing, friendly dogs. They get along well with children and make good family pets.

An English
springer spaniel

45

What Is a Cocker Spaniel?

Another member of the spaniel family is the cocker spaniel. There is an English cocker spaniel breed and an American cocker spaniel. The two breeds are closely related.

Cocker spaniels were bred as hunting dogs. They gained the name "cocker" because they were good at hunting birds called woodcocks. American cockers stand about 15 inches (38 centimeters) tall at the shoulder. They are smaller than golden retrievers or English springer spaniels.

Most cocker spaniels today are family pets. They are usually cheerful, sweet family dogs that like children. Like other sporting dogs, cocker spaniels need regular exercise and like to be outdoors. They also need to have their thick, furry coats groomed regularly.

An American
cocker spaniel

What Is a Labrador Retriever?

The ancestors of Labrador retrievers were from Europe, but the breed assumed its present form on the island of Newfoundland, off the coast of Labrador in eastern Canada.

Labs are usually intelligent, loyal, good-natured, and loving. Because of these qualities, Labs have often been used as guide dogs for the blind and as helpers to other disabled people (see page 40).

Labs are big dogs, just a little taller and heavier than goldens. The American Kennel Club standards state that a lab should be between 21 ½ and 24 ½ inches (54.5 and 62 centimeters) tall at the shoulder.

Labs are easier to groom than many other sporting dogs because they have short hair. Some of the dogs in this breed are yellowish in color, but others are black or chocolate-brown.

48

A chocolate-brown
Labrador retriever

49

What Is an Irish Setter?

The Irish setter is another sporting dog. Like the golden retriever, the Irish setter has long hair with feathering at its chest, belly, legs, and tail. However, unlike the golden, the Irish setter has a longer neck, feathering on its ears, and its coat is a shade of red.

The Irish setter is thinner than a golden. The American Kennel Club states that the ideal size for an Irish setter is between 25 and 27 inches (64 to 69 centimeters) tall at the shoulder.

Irish setters tend to love children. These dogs usually make good family pets. Some Irish setters, however, can be high-strung (nervous). Like many other sporting dogs, Irish setters need regular exercise and careful, frequent grooming.

An Irish setter

What Is a
Dog Show Like?

Dog shows allow owners to prove how wonderful their dog is. At shows, dogs may be judged on how closely their physical traits conform to (match) the standards set by such groups as the American Kennel Club (AKC). Or, a dog may be judged on how well it follows commands in obedience trials or on how well it performs tasks in field trials. The American Kennel Club and the Golden Retriever Club of America (GRCA) are among the many groups that sponsor events.

The American Kennel Club has a program designed to help young people learn how to show dogs. Youth from 9 years through 17 years of age can show a dog in the AKC's Junior Showmanship categories. Juniors can compete in different types of events, including shows that judge their dog's conformity to breed standards or its level of training at obedience trials.

A golden retriever
at a dog show

53

Are There Dangers to Dogs Around the Home?

Dogs can stumble into plenty of danger at home. Here are some things to watch out for.

Make sure that the windows in your home are not open wide enough for a dog to get through. An excited dog could jump right through the screen.

Never give a dog a toy that wasn't made for dogs. Your dog could chew and shred it and might choke on the small pieces. Special tennis balls made for dogs are safer for your pet.

Common causes of serious poisoning in dogs are chemicals intended for such pests as rats and antifreeze that is used in cars. Be careful in any area, such as alleys and around garbage cans, where poisons may have been placed to kill pests. And, antifreeze from a car can be very toxic to dogs; its sweet taste makes dogs really enjoy its flavor. Do not let your dog drink from puddles.

Follow this rule: If you don't know what it is or whether it's harmful—don't let your dog eat it, drink it, or chew on it.

A golden at home

55

What Are Some Common Signs of Illness in Sporting Dogs?

A dog can't tell you, "I feel sick"—at least not in so many words. But dogs do give clues about how they're feeling. A dog that isn't interested in eating may be saying that it doesn't feel well. After all, eating is usually a high point of a dog's day.

One common health problem in golden retrievers is hip dysplasia (an abnormal development of the hip that can be passed down from a parent to offspring). In hip dysplasia, two large bones do not meet properly at the hip joint. As a result, one of the bones sometimes pops out of the joint. Signs of hip dysplasia can include difficulty when walking or running. Some dogs with hip dysplasia can have an operation to fix the problem.

If you see any signs in your dog that something is wrong, make an appointment with your veterinarian.

A golden feeling unwell

What Routine Veterinary Care Is Needed?

Your dog must be healthy to be happy. To stay healthy, it needs regular medical checkups with a veterinarian. Your family needs to find a vet you can all be comfortable with.

When you take your dog for a checkup, the vet will do a physical exam. That means he or she will check the dog's body for signs of possible problems. The vet will also make sure that your dog has regular vaccinations (shots). A vaccine is a special medicine that protects people, dogs, and other animals from certain serious diseases.

The vet will help you keep your dog free of parasites, such as fleas, ticks, and ear mites. These parasites make your dog uncomfortable. They can also spread diseases.

Experts say that a dog should have a complete checkup with a vet every year.

An exam

59

What Are Your Responsibilities as an Owner?

Responsibility is a kind of promise to do something. When you get a dog, you take on responsibilities to your pet. You promise to give the dog love and keep it healthy and safe. That includes making sure the dog is properly fed, exercised, and taken to the veterinarian when needed for any illnesses or injuries.

Another responsibility of owning a dog is to have a vet spay or neuter that dog so the animal will not be able to produce puppies. (A vet spays female dogs and neuters male dogs.) Thousands of unwanted puppies are born every year.

Owners should also make certain their dog receives the necessary vaccinations (shots). That may include a vaccination against rabies, a terrible, painful disease that can be deadly.

A golden puppy gets
veterinary care

Sporting Dog Fun Facts

→ Scientists believe that dogs can see colors beyond black, gray, and white. But, it is likely that dogs cannot see as many colors or as bright a colors as humans do. That's because dogs have fewer cones—the cells in the eye that are sensitive to color.

→ In the mid-1970's, the "first dog" of the United States was a golden retriever, Liberty, who belonged to the family of U.S. President Gerald R. Ford. Liberty lived in the White House between 1974 and 1977.

→ Dogs have a great sense of smell. Most humans have only 5 million smell-receptor cells—cells in the nose that take in and react to smells. Dogs, however, have hundreds of millions of smell-receptor cells. The champion smeller is the bloodhound—with around 300 million receptor cells!

→ The composer Richard Wagner (1813–1883) wrote music only when his Cavalier King Charles spaniel, Peps, was present. Wagner revised music based on the dog's reactions to it. When Peps died, Wagner got a new "musical" dog of the same breed, which he named Fips.

Glossary

breed To produce animals by carefully selecting and mating them for certain traits. Also, a group of animals having the same type of ancestors.

breeder A person who breeds animals.

feathering In some breeds of dog, the unusually long hair that appears in certain areas, such as at the back of the legs or on the tail.

game Wild animals, including birds or fish, hunted or caught for sport or for food.

grooming The act of combing and brushing dogs.

litter The young animals produced by an animal at one birthing.

neuter To operate on a male animal to make it unable to produce young.

pack A number of animals of the same kind hunting or living together. Also a group of dogs kept together for hunting.

parasite An organism (living creature) that feeds on and lives on or in the body of another organism, often causing harm to the being on which it feeds.

purebred An animal whose parents are known to have both belonged to one breed.

rabies A disease caused by a virus that destroys a part of the brain and almost always causes death. Rabies is transmitted by the bite of an animal that has the disease.

shed To throw off or lose hair or fur.

spay To operate on a female animal to make it unable to have young.

trait A feature or characteristic particular to an animal or breed of animals.

Index

For more information about Golden Retrievers and Other Sporting Dogs, try these resources:

The Complete Dog Book for Kids, by the American Kennel Club, Howell Books, 1996

The Golden Retriever Handbook, by D. Caroline Coile, Barron's Educational Series, 2000

Superpuppy: How to Choose, Raise, and Train the Best Possible Dog for You, by Daniel Manus Pinkwater, Clarion Books, revised edition, 2002

The Ultimate Golden Retriever, by Valerie Foss, Howell Books, 2nd edition, 2003

http://www.akc.org/
http://www.canadiangoldens.com/rescue.cgi
http://www.ckc.ca/en/
http://www.grca.org/default.htm
http://www.grcc.net/

Dog Classification

Scientists classify animals by placing them into groups. The animal kingdom is a group that contains all the world's animals. Phylum, class, order, and family are smaller groups. Each phylum contains many classes. A class contains orders, an order contains families, and a family contains genuses. One or more species belong to each genus. Each species has its own scientific name. Here is how the animals in this book fit into this system.

Animals with backbones and their relatives (Phylum Chordata)
Mammals (Class Mammalia)
Carnivores (Order Carnivora)

Dogs and their relatives (Family Canidae)

Domestic dog . . . .*Canis familiaris*